Daniel Fuller Appleton

The Origin of the Maine Law and of Prohibitory Legislation

Daniel Fuller Appleton

The Origin of the Maine Law and of Prohibitory Legislation

ISBN/EAN: 9783743424005

Manufactured in Europe, USA, Canada, Australia, Japa

Cover: Foto ©Suzi / pixelio.de

Manufactured and distributed by brebook publishing software
(www.brebook.com)

Daniel Fuller Appleton

The Origin of the Maine Law and of Prohibitory Legislation

THE ORIGIN

OF

THE MAINE LAW

AND OF

PROHIBITORY LEGISLATION,

WITH A BRIEF MEMOIR OF

JAMES APPLETON.

NEW YORK:
THE NATIONAL TEMPERANCE SOCIETY AND PUBLICATION HOUSE,
58 READE STREET.
1886.

INTRODUCTION.

The origin of the latest, and possibly, of the conclusive measure in the temperance reformation, is a question certainly of some historical importance, and, to all engaged in that movement, one of peculiar interest. To determine this point beyond all controversy is the object of this brief Memoir of my father, written by a friend. Appended to this is the documentary evidence, now gathered together for the first time, that the earliest effort for the prohibition of all traffic in ardent spirits, as a customary beverage, was made by JAMES APPLETON, first as a private citizen in 1832, and then as a member of the Maine Legislature in 1837.

I had been told by my father of the existence of this evidence ; but had not thought it necessary to search for and publish it, until the appearance, lately, of a book which assumes to be a complete history of the temperance movement in this country. In that volume there is no mention either of my father's name or of his services to the temperance cause. As I know that both are familiar to some of those who contributed to the contents of the book, I propose to do what I can to protect his memory against what appears to be an attempt to suppress the truth of history.

To find copies of the documents herewith published, required a long and diligent search in which I was singularly favored by the aid of the Hon. CALEB FOOTE, the senior-editor of the *Salem Gazette*, and of his associate editor, the Hon. N. A. HORTON. In the old volumes of that journal I knew that some of these papers would be found; and it was fortunate for me that Mr. FOOTE, who has been connected with the *Gazette* for sixty-nine years, was familiar with its columns for so long a period, was warmly interested in the object of my search, and, remembering my father as an occasional writer for the *Gazette*, knew very nearly when the papers I was looking for were published.

D. F. APPLETON.

IPSWICH, MASS., *Sept.* 15, 1886.

MEMOIR.

Among those who have done good and signal
service in the cause of temperance, the name of the
late James Appleton of Massachusetts should be
held most gratefully and most tenaciously in remem-
brance by all who have faith in the expediency and
the necessity of a Prohibitory Liquor Law. It was
he who first publicly maintained—as most, if not all,
who believe in Total Abstinence now maintain is the
logical outcome of the Temperance movement—that
legislation has nothing whatever to do with moral
evil except to aim at its complete suppression. If
this is to be the legislative policy of the future as to
the traffic in intoxicating drinks, as it already is
that of several of the States, it is interesting to trace
that policy to its source and to learn something of
the man who first promulgated it.

James Appleton was born in 1786 on the farm in
Ipswich, Massachusetts, granted to his ancestor,
Samuel Appleton, in 1636; to this home he re-
turned in his old age, when the work of his life was
finished, and there he died in 1862. For many years
his home was in the neighboring town of Marblehead,
and for twenty years from 1833 to 1853, he resided
in Portland, Maine. But wherever he lived he was
known and esteemed for his interest and energy in
public affairs, and was looked up to as a born leader
of men. Though a Federalist in politics, he gave his
services, as colonel of a regiment, to his country when

it became involved in a second war with England in 1812. Those old enough to remember the earlier days of the Anti-Slavery movement, if they know anything about it or those engaged in it, will recall the name of General Appleton as conspicuous in that little band of men and women, who, like their great leader, would not equivocate, who would not retreat a single inch, who would be heard, and who were not afraid. Nor was he less earnest in upholding the saving grace of Total Abstinence from all intoxicating drinks; but that doctrine even half a century ago, had so grown into popular favor that the most zealous on its behalf were not easily distinguished in the multitude of its apostles, nor has the memory of them been so carefully preserved. It is, nevertheless, a rather remarkable fact that the documents herewith submitted should have escaped for fifty years the searching eyes of so many writers and speakers, who have sought with unwearied diligence for every possible argument and every historical illustration that could strengthen their appeals to conscience and to common sense against the most direct and fruitful source of degradation, wretchedness, and crime in modern civilization.

The official report of the Centennial Temperance Convention, held at Philadelphia in 1885, a volume of about 650 pages entitled 100 YEARS OF TEMPERANCE, is meant to be, no doubt, the final authority upon this subject, as well as an exhaustive history of the great reform. The Convention was called Centennial because in 1785 Dr. Benjamin Rush, of Philadelphia, published a pamphlet the title of which was, THE

EFFECTS OF ARDENT SPIRITS ON THE HUMAN BODY AND MIND. The publication was not followed by any perceptible immediate results ; no distinctive Temperance Society was formed till nearly twenty-five years afterward, and those who formed it had, perhaps, never heard of Dr. Rush's pamphlet. But the aim of the pamphlet nevertheless foreshadowed the earliest aspect the reform presented about the close of the first decade of this Century ; and those who called the Centennial Convention deemed its publication, a hundred years ago, of so much importance, and of so much historical value,as to be properly recognized as the beginning of the movement whose progress for the century they proposed to commemorate. That they were right can not be questioned. Whether Dr. Rush saw the consequences that would follow, in years to come, the acceptance of the truths he taught ; however much or little he may have imbued his own generation with the zeal with which he was filled upon so novel a subject, he is none the less to be honored that just then, when all men's minds were busy with the great political problems of that thoughtful and pregnant time, he should have brought up for consideration this great social question and have insisted upon its vast importance to human welfare.

Dr. Rush's essay, it is true, would by no means satisfy a modern reformer. Drunkenness and its lamentable consequences he attributed almost solely to the use of ardent spirits, by which he says, "I mean those liquors only which are obtained by distillation from fermented substances of any kind.'

Fermented liquors, wine, cider and beer, he thought, "can seldom be drunken in sufficient quantities to produce intoxication" without exciting such disgust in the offender as to forbid a repetition of the indulgence; and that they were, "moreover, when taken in a moderate quantity, generally innocent, and often have a friendly influence upon health and life." So far as he went, however, he was very much in earnest, and as he devoted a good deal of time to impress upon legislative and religious bodies his views of the evil done by the use of ardent spirits, the publication of his pamphlet might with perfect propriety be taken as a centennial epoch.

The last decade has been a period of centennial commemorations, and that, possibly, may have influenced the selection of one of its years for an imposing temperance celebration. Could any other number than a century of years have answered the same purpose, it might have been remembered that just half a century earlier (1735), James Oglethorpe procured from the British Parliament an act prohibiting the importation of ardent spirits into his colony of Georgia. His efforts to enforce this law proved as unsuccessful as Dr. Rush's exhortations, though, in the one case as in the other, the moral influence of an earnest endeavor can not be accurately measured. Those, however, who proposed, a century or more afterward, to fix a temperance epoch may have felt themselves quite free to take a hundred years, rather than a hundred and fifty, as their point of departure. The popular mind had been aroused to much enthusiasm by Centennial celebrations and might not so readily respond to the longer period. This consideration might have had its influence upon the gentlemen who called the Philadelphia Convention, even if they had remembered how decisive a measure Governor Oglethrope had attempted to enforce for the good of his colonists.

But whether Oglethorpe was forgotten, or whether the members were not familiar with his history, it can hardly be doubted that General Appleton was not heard of in the Philadelphia convention simply because, with one or two marked exceptions, they were absolutely ignorant of how strong his title is to be remembered as a pioneer in the temperance movement. Had it been otherwise the very coincidences of dates would have directed attention to the man who was the first to discern and press on to that culmination of the reform toward which all earlier labor tended and at which all later efforts distinctly aim. Some person curious in such coincidences would hardly have failed to observe that as it was in 1736 James Oglethorpe brought from England his radical measure for the protection of his Georgia colonists, so it was just a century after his failure to enforce the law that James Appleton, as chairman of a legislative committee to which had been referred a petition in regard to the license laws of Maine, made a report, herewith published, which would in time be recognized as the beginning of a new and auspicious era in the temperance reform. Its argument was that inasmuch as "it is now ascertained, not only that the traffic is attended with most appalling evils to the community, but that ardent spirit is entirely useless—that

it is an *unmitigated evil*," the committee, therefore, were
" not only of opinion that the law giving the right to
sell ardent spirits should be repealed, but that a law
should be passed to *prohibit* the traffic in them, except so far as the arts or the practice of medicine
may be concerned." As it was thus a century from
the Oglethorpe law to the Appleton Report, so also
Rush's pamphlet came in just half way between them ;
and the centennial of the publication of Rush's pamphlet was, also, within a few months, the centennial of
the birth of General Appleton. This periodicity of
notable events in the Temperance movement, to which
the Appleton Report is the key-stone, could not have
escaped comment, had the report itself, the harbinger
of nearly all subsequent effectual effort, been made
known to that convention.

But the legislative report, though the most complete, was not the earliest attempt made by General
Appleton for the suppression by law of all traffic in
ardent spirits. It is remembered in his family that he
dated his convictions upon the subject from the year
1831. It came to him—when listening to an earnest
debate, in the Massachusetts Legislature, of which
body he had been a member—as a sudden revelation,
as a discovery in morals, that the way to stop intemperance was to stop it. If the drinking of spirits
was always wrong and dangerous, and the source
of all the monstrous evils charged to it, then it
was not to be tolerated, nor dallied with by license
laws, but put an end to. If there was no liquor there
would be no drunkenness ; if the sale was made il-
legal, the traffic in it and the use of it would become

disgraceful as well as dangerous. It might not, indeed, be possible to suppress it altogether and at once by act of the Legislature ; but as an argument this was just as true of the laws against murder, arson, forgery, theft, or any other acknowledged crime, which bad men would still commit in defiance of the law.

Though persuaded in his own mind that he had discovered the true remedy for the monstrous evil, the first application he proposed was tentative and indirect. Not that he wanted faith in the perfect efficacy of that remedy, but he doubted if the public mind was yet ready for heroic treatment. Accordingly he prepared a petition to the Massachusetts Legislature— this was before he removed to Portland, and when he was residing at Marblehead—praying that the sale of liquor in any quantity less than thirty gallons be forbidden by law.

The proposition was clearly meant as the first step toward absolute prohibition ; indeed, there was no pretence in the petition of concealing the hope of its author that a limitation of the sale of ardent spirits to a minimum of thirty gallons would take from the large majority of drunkards all chance of getting drunk. The purchase of rum in so large a quantity would be beyond their means ; while the moderate drinker who could afford it, would easily and almost unconsciously abandon a habit, unless very firmly fixed, which called for more forethought and larger immediate outlay than the gratification was worth.

But even this compromise aroused more opposition than, probably, General Appleton was prepared for.

The agent of the Massachusetts Temperance Society, a Rev. Mr. Hildreth, pounced upon it at once, as a mischievous measure. His notion evidently was that among the "inalienable rights" of man was the right to rum. He fairly represented the timid public opinion of that day which, in the temperance, as in the anti-slavery, movement, shrunk from any denunciation in "harsh language" of a popular wrong, and from any proposed remedy that would be pronounced "radical." "Moral suasion" was the cant phrase of the time, and if there were a few tender souls—Mr. Hildreth may have been one of them— who used the term in its true sense, with the multitude it only meant that they would not tolerate any onslaught upon evil which reflected upon respectable sinners, was likely to open their eyes and bring them to repentance.

The letter of Mr. Hildreth, and that of another writer, who signs himself "Danvers," are republished herewith to show the spirit in which General Appleton's moderate proposal was met. He was quick to reply whether to argument or cavil, and in three clear and forcible letters, signed "Essex," which we copy from the *Salem Gazette*, of February, 1832, he sets forth his reasons for the faith that is in him, and the real object he had in view in the petition. On one point, however, he acknowledged his error and accepted, in his own way, the rebuke of his opponents. He ought not, he confessed, to have asked the Legislature for a limitation in the traffic in ardent spirits, whether to thirty gallons or any other quantity. The trade, it was plain to him now, should be, not regulated, but prohibited. The opposition he had aroused was an evidence of the foolishness of any proposed compromise between right and wrong. He meant prohibition and ought to have said so directly, rather than have condescended to an expedient which pleased nobody and would deceive but few. "I made a great mistake!" he said to a member of his own family—"a great mistake!" and this he publicly reiterates, it will be observed, in a postscript to his third and final letter—"we wish the prayer of the petition had been without any qualification; for its authors, we believe, intended the absolute prohibition of the traffic, as their argument abundantly evinces." But here was the end of the matter. Perhaps he had gained all he had hoped for in provoking some discussion of the subject, and it is doubtful if the petition, which, probably, nobody but himself would have signed, was ever presented to the Legislature.

Here for the first time prohibitory legislation was proposed, though with no other immediate result. apparently, than to convince its author that the opposition to it would be formidable if not insurmountable. He may have been, for a time discouraged, but he was not defeated. He knew he was right; and he had learned, moreover, a lesson of practical value. If ever again he could make an opportunity to urge his principles upon any legislative body. there should be no mistake of a want of directness in his method.

Meanwhile he had removed to Portland, and in 1836 he was elected a member of the Maine Legisla-

ture. The opportunity he had waited for came when
a petition on the license laws was referred to a Committee of which he was chairman. He could speak
now with a certain authority, and did not need, even
were he so minded, to appeal to public attention by the
suggestion of an indirect and experimental measure.
The whole subject was, no doubt, much clearer in his
mind than when he put forth his thirty gallons petition, and he was ready to meet the unbelieving or
the timid at all possible points of difficulty or objection. He covers the ground so completely, presents his argument so frankly, confidently and
forcibly, that the report might go before any State
Legislature to-day as an exhaustive presentation of
the whole question of Prohibition.

The report of course, was laid upon the table, and
it is not remembered whether it gave rise to any debate. Very likely not; for doubtless to most, if not
all, of the honorable members, it seemed as pre-
posterous as it was novel, and not even worth talking
about. Nevertheless "The Maine Law" was born
then and there, though it was not till nine years later
that the first tentative act was passed as the beginning of prohibitory legislation. The years of agita-
tion and discussion which preceded and prepared the
way for legislation also had a beginning, and there
is neither record, nor tradition, nor memory of the
oldest inhabitant that can trace it beyond the
Appleton Report to the Maine Legislature of 1836-7,
unless it be to the Appleton petition to the Massachusetts Legislature of 1832. But both came from
the same man, and together they leave nothing more

to be said as to the question of the origin of this special temperance policy. James Appleton, as a private citizen of Massachusetts, publicly suggested in 1832, the wisdom of a prohibitory liquor law ; and in 1837 the same James Appleton, as a member of the Maine Legislature, urged upon that body the enactment of such a law. When at last, in 1851, the "Maine Law," as it now stands upon the statute-books of the State, was passed, it was a fitting recognition of his early devotion to the principle of prohibition that he, among others, snould have been called upon to aid in the preparation of the Act.[1]

He lived to see ten years of the enforcement of the perfected law in Maine and in other States. It was, in spirit and purpose, of his own devising, and he would sometimes speak at his own fireside with natural pride and profound thankfulness of the result of his work. But he left it to others to show at some future time how much was due to his fore-sight, his keen moral sense, and his courage. Properly, the historical fact should have come to light in the National Centennial Convention of 1885; but failing that, the documents establishing it are here, for the first time, gathered together for submission to all temperance people to whom the origin of the doctrine of Prohibition must needs be of profound interest.

---

1 *History of the Anti-Slavery Cause in State and Nation.* By Austin Willey. p 374. Portland, 1886.

THE PETITION OF 1832:

PROPOSED SUPPRESSION OF ALL RETAIL TRAFFIC IN ARDENT SPIRITS.

— — ——

LETTER OF THE REV. MR. HILDRETH.

From the " Salem Mercury," Feb. 15, 1832.

To the Friends of Temperance Societies and Temperance Measures:

I have received a printed petition addressed to the Legislature of this Commonwealth and asking for a law to be passed prohibiting the "sale of ardent spirits in a less quantity than thirty gallons." From what source the petition came does not appear; but it was accompanied by a written note, requesting that I would obtain as many signatures as possible, and forward them to the Legislature. I suppose many other friends of temperance societies and temperance measures will receive the petition with its anonymous accompaniment; and therefore, I feel it to be my duty as a known and active friend of temperance, to give my opinion thus publicly of the measure it proposes.

I would previously remark, however, that I am somewhat at a loss to determine whether the person, or persons, that have been instrumental in printing and circulating the petition, are friends or enemies to the temperance cause. From the concealment of their names, and the wild measure they propose, I should rather conclude they are enemies; that they are laying a plan to make the friends of temperance societies and temperance measures appear extravagant and ridiculous, by inducing us to ask for what every sensible man knows we cannot obtain.

But if the petition has been printed and circulated, as I am inclined to think is the case, by those who really wish that all trade in ardent spirits, as articles of diet, should come to an end, then I am very sorry that the persons who have thus undertaken to promote the adoption of measures so important, are not better informed as to the real state of public opinion. It is true that great and pleasing changes have taken place in the commonwealth at large, relative to the use of ardent spirits; and we are encouraged to hope, that the time is coming on when it will cease to be regarded by any person of sound mind and good habits, as an article of living—as either a necessary or a comfort of life. But from the best information I have been able to collect, public opinion is in great need of further improvement on this subject; many worthy, and respectable, and influential men still take *alcohol*, under the impression that it does them good; many industrious and hard-working men take it under the false impression that it makes them stronger for toil; and so many of almost all pursuits and callings in the various parts of the commonwealth, especially in the parts bordering on the seaboard, are still in the habit of *taking a little*, that I am persuaded the paramount duty of the friends of temperance is, not to petition the Legislature, but to go on in their way of enlightening the public mind, as they have been doing in years past. If we are not wanting in prudence, energy, and perseverance, we shall in good time succeed, as I trust, in bringing our fellow citizens almost universally to the same opinion and practice which we are maintaining, relative to the use of ardent spirit. But I am satisfied. more hurt than good would be done by sending the proposed petition to the Legislature the present session. There is full enough of excitement there already, touching the matter of *vending :* and for one, I am not for fanning the coals. I would heartily concur in any judicious measures for still further improvement of public opinion, and for altering by means of the truth, instead of the strong arm of the law, the habits of those who still make use of ardent spirits as an article of diet, either because they *love* it, or because they think it beneficial. The passage of such a law as the petition proposes, would, in effect, do away all regulations concerning the sale of ardent spirits; for in the present state of public opinion it would entirely be disregarded by those who are making money by selling rum. I sincerely hope no friends of temperance societies or temperance measures will sign the petition.

H. HILDRETH,
Agent of the Massachusetts Society for the
Suppression of Intemperance.

GLOUCESTER, *Feb.* 9, 1832.

MR. HILDRETH SUSTAINED.

From the " Salem Gazette," Feb. 17, 1832.

GENTLEMEN :

I read with much satisfaction the communication of the Rev. H. Hildreth, of Gloucester, in the *Mercury* of Wednesday last, in relation to a certain form of Memorial to the Legislature, on the sale of ardent spirits, which has been circulated in this community. Whence this Memorial originated, I do not know;—but that it has been widely disseminated is apparent, from the facts stated by Mr. Hildreth; and the further facts, that several copies of the same have been received by gentlemen in this town, with a request that they would procure subscriptions, and forward the same to the Legislature.

The prayer of this Memorial is, that the Legislature would pass a law "prohibiting the sale of ardent spirits in this Commonwealth, in a less quantity than *thirty gallons*, &c." It may well be doubted whether a petition so extraordinary originated with the friends or enemies of temperance. But wherever it originated, it is exceedingly coarsely drawn up, and wild in its object.

That the regulation of the sale of ardent spirits is a very proper subject to engage the attention of our Legislature, I readily admit; and that much good may be effected by having judicious laws on the subject, and having them faithfully observed, I also grant;—but a law of the character prayed for would be a mere *nullity*,—or if it had any effect at all, it would be to furnish the drunkard with an ample supply for his appetite.

If you would correct by law, the evil of intemperance—let drunkenness be punished as a *crime* : and let those accessory, in aiding or abetting the same, by furnishing the means or in any other manner, be subjected to severe penalties for so doing. And let drunkenness in the *higher* as well as in the *lower* classes of society be punished also. Let no man, who is ever proved guilty of being drunk, whether he be *high* or *low*, *rich* or *poor*, *honorable* or *not honorable*, be admitted to hold any office of honor, trust, or profit, in the community. Surely such a man is not fit to hold any office—then why should he be suffered to hold it? I have no allusion to any public officer —I speak of the principle generally—but would you correct the evils of intemperance in the *lower* classes, you must begin your reformation in the *higher*. While drunkenness is not censured in the *Hotel* and the *Palace*, you never can banish it from the Grog-shop and the *Hovel*.

Let me add one word upon the plan proposed in our Legislature of vesting the power of granting licenses for the sale of ardent spirits in the boards of Selectmen of the respective towns. Such a measure, in my opinion, would be most unfortunate —would be a *curse* to the community. Let this be so—and the only criterion in the choice of these officers would be—will they favor or will they oppose the selling rum. And notwithstanding the change that has been effected in public opinion, in regard to the necessity of the use of ardent spirits, in most of our towns. I fear, now and for a long time to come, there will be found a majority who are in favor of the *people's rights*, as they are pleased to term it— who are in favor of no restrictions upon trade—who are disposed *now* and *then to take a little*, for their stomach's sake and often infirmities.

DANVERS.

No. 1.

THE PETITION.

From the "Salem Gazette." Feb. 21, 1832.

MESSRS. EDITORS:

We regretted to notice in your last the communication of the Rev. Mr. Hildreth; for beside that it was uncalled for, it cannot fail of an unfavorable bearing on the cause for which he is an "agent." So far as our observation extends, the friends of temperance regret its appearance, while the enemies speak of it in the strong language of approbation. The most prominent feature of that communication is the egregious vanity of the writer. "I feel it to be my duty," says he, "I am very sorry," "I would heartily concur," &c.—precisely as though the responsibility of every measure devolved on him, and as though every one was dependent on his judgment for their opinions. The Rev. "agent," complains that the authors of the Petition, to which he refers, *concealed* their names. It is true that the Petition was sent without any authority from names, because the authors trusted that every gentlemen to whom it was sent, was competent to judge for himself of its merits. No number of names could have made its facts more true, nor the reasoning more conclusive; nor is the wisdom or the folly of his address more certain, because the Rev. "agent" appended his name to it.—His office may possibly give dignity, but it confers no authority, much less does it impart either prudence or wisdom.

The manner in which the Rev. " agent " has thought proper to speak of the Petition and its authors, is as illiberal as it was unprovoked. The Petition is pronounced a " wild measure," " extravagant and rediculous." At one time the Rev., " agent " is at " a loss to determine whether the persons who gave circulation to the Petition are enemies or friends to the temperance cause ;" at another time he "concludes they are enemies ;" and then again he is " inclined to think they really wish an end to ardent spirits ! " Really, the gentleman was most unfortunate, in not determining in his own judgment, the purpose of the Petition, before he ventured to prescribe for the conduct of others. We here give an extract from the Petition, that your readers may see and judge for themselves, how little reason he had for the use of such language ·

" It has been found by the friends of this cause that the laws of this Commonwealth, authorizing Licenses to taverners and retailers to sell ardent spirits, oppose an insuperable obstacle to its progress. For beside the difficulty of dissuading from a practice which has for its support the authority of the commonwealth, the laws assume that the sale and use of ardent spirits, to a certain extent at least, are of public benefit and necessity and promotive of individual advantage and happiness. This assumption, your petitioners humbly apprehend, has been ascertained to be utterly unsupported and unfounded; and if it were possible to separate from our associations long continued habit and universal practice in the commonwealth, it is believed that a license to disseminate the small-pox would *be thought to be not less proper and reasonable than a license to sell ardent spirits ; for there is no reason for supposing that the mortality, or other evils resulting from the former, would be greater than what by careful examination has been found to result from the latter.   In the United States it has been estimated, that thirty-five thousand victims fall annually into their graves by intemperance.   But this is only a portion of the evil ; for three-quarters of the pauperism and crimes may be traced to this source ; and to these may be added an amount of suffering and degradation and wretchedness which exceeds all human computation.   All these evils are justly ascribed to the legalized traffic in ardent spirits, or rather to the want of a law to prohibit their sale altogether.   And it may be further observed, that the use of ardent spirits is not, as is true in many other cases, a substantial good, yet liable to be abused, but it is in all respects an unmitigated evil, having no redeeming properties whatever ; and the total prohibition of its sale would not, in the opinion of your petitioners, be permanently injurious to any individual or detrimental to any of the interests of the State."*

We ask the attention of the Rev. "agent" again to this Petition, and let him specify the objectionable passages.   Will it be said that the "public mind must be enlightened" before the measure contemplated can succeed? Be it so ; but has he yet to learn that petitioning the Legislature is one mode, and a very proper mode too, for securing this object ? It is believed that public opinion is already in advance of the law on this important subject ; but it must be added that so long as the Commonwealth enters into a sort of contract, with more than two thousand individuals, making it their interest, and in some sense their duty, for the *public good*, to sell ardent spirits in every town in the State, the public mind never will be properly enlightened on this question. It was, therefore, thought quite time for the friends, some of them at least, to state openly and fearlessly the fallacy and the evil of the whole License System; and to show that it is founded on premises that are utterly untenable and false. Does the Rev. agent not know that a bill is now pending before the Legislature, the object of which is to open the door still wider, and to facilitate the sale and use of ardent spirits? Now it was one object of this petition to arrest this bill by showing that the only proper legislation on this subject, is to prohibit their sale altogether. All right reasoning, on the temperance question, necessarily leads to this conclusion; and it is not doubted that this principle will soon obtain, if it is not retarded by the half-way policy and indecision of those who ought to be " better informed."

But the gentleman would not appeal to the " strong arm of the law;" now it is the object of the petition to point out the proper object for which this " strong arm " should be raised. It should shut the door against instead of opening it to intemperance. It is this " strong arm of the law " that has opened tippling shops in every corner and village of the State; and we ask, if this " strong arm " is raised at all, that it may be raised to save and not to destroy.

We do not know that an act to prohibit the sale of ardent spirits, would put a stop at once to vending it; but then, we think, every one will agree that whatever be the power of the law, it should be exerted to prevent and not to protect the traffic in it. If there be any virtue in legislative enactments, it should lend its aid not to encourage but to discountenance and prevent intemperance. As the law now is, the selectmen in the several towns are virtually obliged, every year, to certify under oath, that the *public good* requires more than two hundred venders of ardent spirits in the County of Essex! With such laws, how can any one expect to suppress intemperance? And the moment we call the public attention to the evil, the Rev. agent calls out, you are " wild," gentlemen, in " the present state of public opinion," to " touch the matter of vending," for " many worthy, and respectable, and influential men, still take a little "—*none to speak of*.

ESSEX.

No. 11.

THE LICENSE SYSTEM.

From the "Salem Gazette," Feb. 24, 1832.

MESSRS. EDITORS:

One of the causes of intemperance, is the law of the Commonwealth granting licenses to sell ardent spirits; and until these laws are radically altered—until the traffic in ardent spirit is absolutely prohibited, no plans or efforts for its suppression can be effectually and permanently successful. These laws are precisely adapted to facilitate the free sale and use of ardent spirit. They make it lawful and reputable for the man who has a license to sell it, and of course not dishonorable to purchase and use it. The statute of 1787 provides that "it shall be the duty of the selectmen in the several towns, annually, to certify to the Court of the General Sessions of the Peace, what number of innholders and retailers, in their respective towns, they judge to be necessary for the *public good:*" and the Justices of the General Sessions of the Peace, in each county, be and they are hereby directed, not to license more persons in any town or district to keep houses for common entertainment, or to retail spirituous liquors, as aforesaid, than the Justices shall judge necessary for the receiving and refreshment of travellers and strangers, and to serve the public occasions of such town or district, or one neccessary for the *public good;* and all public houses shall be on or near the high streets, roads, and places of great resort."

Here the law implicitly asserts the usefulness of ardent spirit, and kindly undertakes to make provision to supply the community with it; and as if to give importance to the article, and respectability to the trader, it further provided that, before any person can obtain a license, the selectmen should recommend him "as a man of sober life and conversation," "and firmly attached to the constitution and laws of this Commonwealth." We are aware that it was the design of the license laws to *regulate* and restrict the sale of ardent spirits, and if you please, to prevent the abuse of it. But our object is not to enquire into the design of the laws, but rather to show their actual tendency, and this we insist has been to favor intemperance, to give it being and continuance. Its chief influence has been to perpetuate the mighty evil to all future generations. It first assumes, what the testimony of numerous distinguished physicians and thousands of others has proved to be false, that spirituous liquors are necessary, and then most humanely makes provision to secure to the inhabitants an abundant supply, by making it the interest of a select few to keep it for sale; and we have yet to learn that the ruinous effects of rum are lessened by the fact that it is sold only by men "of sober life and conversation."

The effects of these laws have been precisely what might have been expected. Two or three thousand shops have been opened in the State, in the most convenient places for supplying the inhabitants with the deadly poison ; and the amount that has been consumed almost exceeds belief. "In one town, containing a population of about one thousand, the quantity of ardent spirits used in one year, was 10,000 gallons, and there were 17 retailers licensed to sell it."

In addition to the miseries of debt and poverty which they entail upon a community, they are the parent of three-quarters of the diseases that prevail, and of the crimes that are committed. "It is ardent spirits that fill our poor-houses and our jails, our penitentiaries, mad-houses, and State prisons. It is ardent spirits that furnish victims for the gallows. They are the greatest curses that God ever inflicted on the world, and may well be called the seven vials of his wrath. They become more destructive in their consequences than war, plague, pestilence or famine, yea, than all combined. They are slow in their march but sure in their grasp. They seize not only on the natural, but the moral man. They consign the body to the tomb and the soul to hell."

The license system has been tried, and we have a right to pronounce it a total failure. The best test of the utility of any law is experience. There is no ground for believing that a greater quantity of ardent spirits would have been consumed, had there been no regulations of its sale whatever. The mere circumstance whether a few or many sold it would have no effect, provided those who were licensed kept sufficient to supply the demand ; and the law has most cautiously guarded against any deficiency. And it has frequently been remarked, that retailers, especially in the country, are careful never to get out of rum, if they have nothing else for their customers. But it is not certain that the number who vend the article is less than it would have been without the law, for it is found that very few, if any, who wish to keep the article, are denied a license. There is no reason, therefore, for supposing that the law, in any view of it, has had the effect to lessen the amount consumed, but on the contrary greatly to increase it. This it has done, by giving character and respectability to the trade; and by proceeding on the false and absurd principle that rum was useful and necessary; and that the *public good* required the traffic. It is morally certain that it has had this effect; for we have seen that the law requires that the bar-room "must be near the place of great public resort," and the vender must be of "sober life and conversation;" and the consequence has been that the tavern is frequently the next door to the meeting-house, and the keepers, in many cases, are the squires and deacons of the parish, for who more distinguished by a sober life and conversation than they—thus making it most suitable and reputable for church members and other "worthy and respectable and influential men" to resort thither on the Sabbath, as well as other days, for the purpose of reviving their languid spirits, and preparing them for the duties and worship of the sanctuary.

ESSEX.

No. III.

ABSOLUTE PROHIBITION PROPOSED

From the "Salem Gazette," Feb. 28, 1832.

MESSRS. EDITORS :

We submitted a few remarks in your last, to show that the license laws had not only failed of limiting or preventing intemperance, but that they had in some measure created and continued the evil. Our first objection to these laws is, that they assert or imply that ardent spirits are useful and that the traffic in them is necessary. Our second objection is, that the manner in which the sale of them is regulated, is suited to give character and respectability to the trade, and of course to increase the traffic and all the tremendous and indescribable evils attendant on it. Our third objection is, that all laws are necessarily of injurious tendency which directly legalize any trade or business which is in itself pernicious and that is not needful to any one interest in the community.

It is now proposed to show not only that these laws should be repealed, but that a law should be passed prohibiting the sale of ardent spirits without any qualification.

1. The present laws should be repealed, because, as already shown, they are useless ; they have had no effect to restrain intemperance, but rather to increase it by making it lawful and respectable to

supply the insidious aliment that keeps it alive. These laws are also a great hindrance to the various moral means which are now in operation to put an end to intemperance. Go to the retailer and beseech him to empty his shop of the vile liquid, and he will tell you "it is his regular lawful business, that he is as much opposed to intemperance as you are, and that he always withholds the cup from the drunkard." You again appeal to his reason, and point him to the consequences of the traffic on all who purchase the article. He again replies, "the law has determined that a certain number of retailers are *necessary to the public good*, that he has paid his fee and got his license in his pocket, and that he cannot be answerable for consequences." It is easy to see that all persuasion will be lost upon him : and we agree, the retailer is right unless the law is wrong. Repeal the laws and grant no licenses, and then every man who sells rum, will do it on his own responsibility. He could not plead the statute, nor throw off the responsibility upon the State ; and the Commonwealth would be free from the unrighteous, guilty traffic.

"The vending of ardent spirits cannot be carried on without guilt. Every grog shop exhibits scenes that religion cannot witness without horror. Here every evil passion is fed! Here is kept the food of drunkenness, and hither resort all those miserable victims of the disease, who would rather die of it than be cured! Here is found the poison that vitiates the taste of the temperate, and prepares them to supply the places of those who die of this plague! Here the temperate drink, and here the temperate learn to be drunkards. All the drunkards in the country are brought up at these stores. They are the schools of intemperance, and as long as they continue the traffic in ardent spirits, they will continue to be the poison of the land. As long as they furnish the supply of ardent spirits called for, they will continue to send forth through the towns in which they are found, a pestilence, laying waste every noble and manly feeling of the human heart, and every lovely trait in the human character. Is not this so? Where were the drunkards of our village formed, but at those places where ardent spirits are sold? Where is the origin of all that poverty and crime which are traced to intemperance, but at these aceldamas of human blood? Where can the wife and the mother find the source of that fountain of tears which they are constrained to shed, but at these fountains of ardent spirits?"

If it is said that among those who vend ardent spirits, there are "many worthy, and respectable, and influential men"; it may be replied, that if it be so, they do not derive their repectability from selling rum, but in spite of it. Formerly, when but little, was said or thought on this subject, the sale and use of ardent spirit involved comparatively very little that was wrong; but now, with all the light which examination and experience have poured on the public mind, it is difficult to see how these practices can consist with innocence. We trust it will not be considered unsuitable if we say, and we say it with all seriousness and reverence, "The times of this ignorance God winked at, but now commandeth all men every where to repent."

A law should be passed prohibiting the sale of ardent spirits. Many are startled, we know, by this proposition. Some, and even an agent for the suppression of intemperance, call it a "wild" scheme. But let us examine it. Why should it not be prohibited? We request any who may be opposed to us, to answer specifically this question, why should it not be prohibited? It has been proved again and again, by competent witnesses, that so far from being valuable to any one purpose, it is the direst calamity that ever visited our world.

Kettredge says : "One gallon for a town, is just four quarts too much."

Aitman : "Art never made so fatal a present to mankind, as the invention of distilling spirituous liquors."

Paris : "The art of distilling must be regarded as the greatest curse ever inflicted on human nature."

Frank : "The use of these liquors ought to be entirely dispensed with, on account of their tendency, even when taken in small doses, to induce disease, premature old age and death."

Munro : "A man has no more need of ardent spirit, than a cow or a horse."

Kirk : "Men who had always been considered temperate had, by using it, shortened life more than twenty years, and that the regular and respectable use of this poison kills more men than drunkeness itself."

Cheyne : "These liquors are most like opium in

their nature and operation, and most like arsenic in their deleterious and poisonous effects."

Sewall : "There is no case in which ardent spirit is indispensible, and for which there is not an adequate substitute."

Warren : "The necessity of using ardent spirits even in medicine is extremely limited. Now and then a solitary instance presents itself, in which there seems to be some reason for preferring alcohol to other articles. In the greater number of cases of disease requiring the use of stimulant liquors, wine is to be preferred to alcohol ; and the importance of this is much less than was thought a few years since."

ESSEX.

The petition which has been frequently referred to, proposed that it should not be sold in a less quantity than thirty gallons. It was supposed that this, in effect, would be a prohibition. We think such an act would so operate, for the very thought of thirty gallons of alcohol would strike most men with horror. But since this is objected to from various quarters, we wish the prayer of the petition had been without any qualification ; for its authors, we believe, intended the absolute prohibition of the traffic, as their argument abundantly evinces.

GENERAL APPLETON'S REPORT,

TO THE MAINE LEGISLATURE OF 1837.

As Chairman of the Committee on License Laws.

— ⬥ —

From the "Temperance Watchman." Portland, Me., Feb. 15, 1853.

[We publish in this number the able report of Gen. Appleton. It was presented to the Legislature of Maine in 1837 ; as an argument, it is complete and cannot fail to convince any man of reflection that it is sound in logic and true in principle. We bespeak for it a careful reading. This is the first announcement of the prohibitory principles, and is the origin of the Maine Law.]

———

The Joint Select Committee to whom was referred the petition of Edward Kent and others have had the same under consideration and ask leave to present the following

REPORT.

A proposition materially to change a system which has for years been incorporated with State Legislation, and which is intimately connected with various important interests of the State, should receive more

than common attention. Impressed with the importance of the subject submitted to them, the committee
have endeavored to present as ample a view of the
question as the time and means which they have at
command would allow.

Laws granting license to sell ardent spirits, have
been enacted in every State in the Union ; and so
far as the Committee know, they are at this time,
under different forms, in operation in every State.
The first license law of Massachusetts was passed in
the year 1646, and although from that time until the
present, they have been variously altered and
changed, yet at this very time, the license laws of
Maine are substantially what they were at first — *they
authorize the sale of ardent spirits for common use.* This
is the principle that gives them character. The
manner of granting the license, or the form of the
law, are circumstances of little or no moment.

These laws, then, have been in active operation
nearly two centuries, and this period seems sufficient
for a full and fair trial ; and what is the history of
this experiment? When the law was first made,
intemperance was of rare occurrence, and was designed, as appears, to prevent rather than cure
the evil. From that time until the temperance reformation, as it is sometimes called, we gradually but
constantly increased in the use of ardent spirits, and
became more and more intemperate, until we were
reproached, by some foreign writers, as a nation of
drunkards. Although other causes, no doubt, were
in operation, yet there are many reasons for the
opinion, that those laws were the principal cause of

he result. They make it lawful and reputable, for the person who has a license to sell it, and of course not improper nor dishonorable to purchase and use it. The law also asserts the necessity and usefulness of ardent spirits, and makes provision that the whole community may be supplied ; and, as if to give importance to the article, and respectability to the traffic, it provides that the vender shall " be of sober life and conversation and of good moral character, and suitably qualified for the employment."

We shall not question that it was the design of the license laws to regulate and restrict the sale of ardent spirits, and even to prevent its abuse ; but our present enquiry is not of the design, but the actual tendency of the law. This, we believe, has been to promote intemperance, to give it being, and to continue it, down to the present time. It first assumes that, which the united testimony of physicians and thousands of others has proved to be false, that alcohol is necessary for common use, and then makes provisions that there shall be no deficiency, by making it the interest of a select few to keep it for sale. The mere circumstance whether few or many keep it for sale is unimportant, provided those who were licensed, kept sufficient to supply the demand. It is the inevitable tendency of the shop and bar-room to decoy men from themselves and their self-control, and our whole experience under the license laws of the State, has proved how hopeless it is that such places should exist and men not become intemperate. If the poison was not freeely offered, and offered for sale under the sanction of law—it could not, it would not be purchased.

The best test of the utility of any law is experience, and by this rule the license law has been most satisfactorily tried; and there is no reason for supposing that the amount of ardent spirits used has been less, but rather that the consumption was much greater in consequence of the law ; for the law has given character and respectability to the traffic, and has done much to fix on the minds of the public, the impression that rum was necessary, and that the public good required it.

Go to the retailer and beseech him to empty his shop of the poison, and he will tell you it is his regular lawful business, that he is as much opposed to intemperance as you are, and that he always withholds the cup from the drunkard. You again appeal to his sympathy, and point him to the consequences of the traffic, on all who use the article. He again replies, that the law has determined that a certain number of retailers are necessary to the *public good*, that he has paid his fee and got his license in his pocket, and that he cannot be answerable for consequences : now it is very plain that the retailer is right, unless the law is wrong. Repeal the present law, and *prohibit* the sale, and then every man, who ventured to sell rum, would be obliged to do it on his own responsibility. He could not plead the statute, nor throw off the reproach upon the State.

It was seen many years since, that no strictness of regulations could prevent abuse or violation of the laws, yet strange as it may appear, the Legislature did not at once prohibit the traffic, but proceeded to cure the mischief by further regulations, under penalties more strict and severe. But these regulations only served to keep alive and augment the evil; and how could it have been otherwise? It is repugnant to the first perceptions of common sense, to suppose that a man, who merely obtained a license could *innocently* sell strong water—the name first given to rum in the colony laws—and that another man could be justly liable to whipping, which was ordered by one act, for selling it without license. The same may be observed of our present laws; they are absurd on the face of them. The people will never be satisfied that if the taverner may rightfully vend the article by the glass, to the ruin of his neighbor, it is criminal for the retailer to do the same.

We, therefore, may consider it settled that all attempts to discriminate between the licensed and unlicensed vender are utterly futile and vain. And as long as it is considered right and proper to grant licences, just so long intemperance will continue to fill our jails and poor houses and penitentiaries. It is not a thing indifferent in itself, whether the traffic be licensed or not, and that it may be made right or wrong by the arbitrary enactments of legislation. The trade, except for medicinal and manufacturing purposes, is morally and politically wrong; and no law or legislation can change its essential character

Complaints are frequently made against our public officers, such as selectmen, &c., that they license too many, and among them many unsuitable persons, and that it is only necessary to enforce the present laws. This complaint is unfounded. The blame attaches to the law, and not to the public officer.

We have no right to expect that selectmen, or other officers will be wiser or better than the law. It is their duty to execute, and not to make or alter the law.

In speaking of the license laws, however, we would by no means reflect improperly upon the character of those who established them. Our fathers were governed by the loftiest patriotism and the sternest moral virtue. They knew the evils and sinfulness of intemperance, and these laws were designed to secure the people against both ; and had they also known that ardent spirits were entirely useless—that a license to vend them would entail on the community, poverty and crime and every evil work—there are strong reasons for believing from what we know of their laws, in other analagous cases, that they would have prohibited the sale entirely.

But they were mistaken in relation to the nature of alcohol : and assumed that it was useful and necessary, and under this mistake they undertook to regulate the traffic in the best way they could. With the present age it is far otherwise. It is now ascertained, not only that the traffic is attended with most appalling evils to the community, but that ardent spirit is entirely useless—that it is *an unmitigated evil.*

This fact—and it is the basis of this report—is certain. It is made out by the strictest scrutiny into the properties of alcohol, and by the experience and observation of thousands in every situation in life, and under circumstances most favorable to an accurate judgment ; and how any man, with the evidence before him which a few past years has supplied, can now question its truth, it is difficult to conceive.

We are placed, therefore, in relation to this subject, in circumstances very different from those which existed when the laws were first made. We have some facts which they who made them did not have. And must the laws remain the same, notwithstanding we have ascertained that they are founded in error? Shall we not alter and frame them to correspond to fact? If it is found that the bar-room and grog-shop are subversive of the public good may, we not say so—*shall we not shut them up*—shall we not cover the fountain whose pestilential streams have spread through all this fair country disease and desolation and death?

The objections, then, to licence laws are these—they assert or imply what is false in point of fact, viz:—that ardent spirit is useful and necessary. 2d. That all laws are necessarily of injurious tendency which directly legalize any trade or business which is in itself destructive of the peace and virtue of society. 3d. That the manner in which the traffic is regulated, is suited to give character and reputation to the trade, and of course to extend its evils far and wide. 4th. These laws oppose an insuperable obstacle to the cause of temperance; so long as these laws exist, just so long intemperance will abound.

Your Committee are not only of opinion that the law giving the right to sell ardent spirits should be repealed, but that a law should be passed to *prohibit* the traffic in them; except so far as the arts or the practice of medicine may be concerned. The reasons for such a law are as numerous as the evils of intemperance. Such a law is required for the same reason that we make a law to prevent the sale of unwholesome meats; or the law for the removal of any nuisance; or any other laws which have for their object to secure the good people of this State in the quiet and peaceable enjoyment of their rights, and against any practice which endangers the health and life of the citizen, or which threatens to subvert our civil rights and overthrow our free government. We would *prohibit* the sale of ardent spirits, because intemperance can never be suppressed without such *prohibition.* There is no more reason for supposing that this evil can be restrained without law, than for supposing you can restrain theft, or gambling, or any other crime without law.

And it seems obvious to remark—and it is presumed that no one will question the correctness of the position—that all legislation, touching this subject, should be of a character to favor and promote temperance and suppress intemperance. That this was the design of the license laws, is readily admitted; but we believe that it has been abundantly shown that this has not been either their effect or tendency. This indeed is so apparent, that it is a common remark that the license laws are the great obstacles to the progress of temperance. Now it appears equally certain that no legislation can have any tendency to prevent intemperance but that which directly *prohibits* the sale. This will be a public expression, by the legislature, which cannot be mistaken, and which cannot fail of exerting the most salutary influence upon the whole community.

No object is more important than life and health; for the security of these, among other things, government is instituted. The laws of God as well as of man hold human life sacred; it cannot be trifled with, or jeopardized with impunity. What object is there more worthy of the Legislature, than laws to preserve the lives and health of the citizens? It is for this end we have health and quarantine laws, which from the value and importance of the object, invest health officers with almost unlimited power; and this is right. Now when it is known, by the observation of all men, that the traffic in any article, entails not only pauperism and crime on the community, but that in numerous cases it shortens human life, and in many instances destroys it at once; it is difficult escaping the conclusion that the government should interpose and *prohibit* it altogether.

The objection will doubtless be made, that if we had such a law it could not be enforced. Now admit' the validity of this objection, and it proves the utter hopelessness of the case; for no one we presume will venture the supposition, that you can accomplish against law, that which you could not effect with it.

It is sufficiently difficult to reform the manners and habits of a community, when the influence and authority of the law can be brought to aid the object, but to do this *against* the law, and against the direct and powerful interest of a numerous class of men, created by the law, is scarcely possible.

But your Committee do not admit that such a law

could not be enforced ; although it is probable there would be many evasions of it. At a time when so many are interested in the subject of temperance, it is impossible that such a law should be generally disregarded. One important effect would be to render the traffic disreputable, as well as unlawful. No individual, who had any respect for his character would continue the practice. There are many respectable dealers, who are now desirous of excluding ardent spirit from their shops, but who under the operation of the present laws, find it almost impracticable so to do ; for by breaking off, they would not only lose the profits of this article, but they would sacrifice no inconsiderable portion of their business in other respects. This is known to be the fact by numerous trials.

Why should the power to execute the law be questioned in this case more than any other ? This is never suggested in respect to any other law that is thought needful for the public welfare ; nor is the objection well founded. But suppose the law we have in view should be sometimes violated ? this would be no sufficient objection to making it ; for what law is there which men keep perfectly ? But we are not left to conjecture on this point. We have a law to prevent gambling in this State ; now the effect of this law has not been to banish gambling from the State ; but it has had the effect to prevent or greatly restrain the evil. It is considered disgraceful to keep a gambling house, and gamblers are unwilling to be known in this character ; hence they seek the darkness of the night and secluded places for their purpose, and the community are generally thus saved from the pernicious influence of their example. Now suppose instead of this law prohibiting gambling, we had a statute to regulate gambling by granting licenses to open gambling shops in every part of the State ; and it would be much less demoralizing, and not more unreasonable than the rum laws; what, your Committee ask, would be the effect of such a law? Can anyone doubt that gambling shops would be as common as retail shops now are ?

It is in vain, therefore, to object to a law that it cannot prevent the offence it prohibits. We have a law against theft, but have we no larcenies? Yet who would be secure in his property, without the law? So it is believed that a law to prevent the sale of ardent spirits, would have the most salutary influence. It would then be as disgraceful to keep a rum shop as a gambling shop. Besides, the mere existence of such a law would exert the most salutary influence on the public mind. It would of itself go to correct public opinion in regard to the necessity of ardent spirits ; for it is not more true that the laws are an expression of public opinion, than that they influence and determine public opinion. They are as truly the cause as the effect of the popular will. It is of the nature of law, to mould the public mind to its requirements, and to fasten upon it an abiding impression of its value and necessity.

It may be objected that we have already tried in numerous cases, to stay the progress of intemperance, by enforcing the law, but that it is found by long experience to be wholly ineffectual. This objection arises from a strange misapprehension of our license law. The fact, we reply, is not true. We have no law against selling rum—we never had a law the most perfect observance of which would have secured this community against intemperance. All our laws, as before observed, authorize the sale and use of the article. The difficulty is not that the law is not enforced; but it is, that when executed it has no tendency to prevent the evil. And we do not complain of the present laws merely that they are imperfect, but they are radically bad—that they are founded on principles totally deceptive and false. The present laws are sufficiently strict and severe, not, however, against selling rum but only against unlicensed venders. They proceed upon the supposition that if men and their families are ruined by the retailed shops—if our prisons are filled with felons and our poor-houses with paupers, it is no great matter, if only it be done according to law.

The truth is, the licence laws do not even as a rule of action, prescribe temperance. In this particular they are an anomaly. All good and wholesome laws, prescribe at least, what is right, and forbid what is wrong. They raise the standard high, and caution, and warn, and forbid; and all who observe them are secure; if their penalty fall on any, it is through their own folly in disregarding the law. Not so with the rum laws, in their spirit and letter whether executed or not executed, whether obeyed or disobeyed, their only effect is to destroy. The path they mark out, is not the path of truth and safety, of virtue and happiness; but it is the highway of deception and anger and tears and wretchedness and blood—it is covered in its whole extent by the mangled and dying, and with the carcasses of dead men—it leads to ruin, and its steps take hold on hell. It may also be objected that the Legislature has no constitutional right to enact a prohibitory law—that it would be oppressive and an encroachment on the rights of the citizens.

The history of our State Government is but the history of measures and expedients, having for their object the security and happiness of the whole people. But no law can be enacted for these objects, which does not, in some form or other, operate as a restraint upon every man in society. We will take only one example. The law of the road is perfectly arbitrary, for there is no reason in the case itself, why a traveler when he meets another, should turn to the right rather than to the left; and yet who denies either the constitutionality or utility of the law? And there are many other statutes which operate to restrain the citizen, in certain actions, which in themselves are not necessarily wrong, but which, unrestrained, might prove detrimental to the interests of the State at large.

But it is too late to deny the right of the Legislature on this subject. It has already in numerous cases legislated on the sale of ardent spirits, and their acts have received the sanction of the highest judicial authorities. What are the present laws, but a prohibition of the traffic to all who do not first obtain a license? It is only necessary to extend the prohibition to every citizen, and the whole object is at once obtained. And it appears evident to the Committee, that if we have any law on the subject, it should be *absolutely prohibitory*. *The trade is a public evil, or it is not: if it is, it is the right and duty of the Legislature to stay it at once; if it is not an evil, it should be equally free to all.*

But the trade in ardent spirits is a public business, carried on in the market places; and if it is found by experience that this business is necessarily ruinous to individuals, and a great public nuisance, there can be no question that it clearly comes within the right of the Legislature to suppress it. We would not prohibit the sale of ardent spirits, because it is inconsistent with our religious and moral obligations —although doubtless this is the fact—but because the traffic is inconsistent with our obligations as citizens of the State, and subversive of our social rights and civil institutions.

But we have yet to learn what authority it is, that would be violated by an act to prohibit the sale of ardent spirits. Not surely the State Constitution, for that has no provision that can be so construed as to limit the Legislature in this matter. Nor the Federal Constitution, unless it is supposed the power to collect a revenue is of this character. But what if Congress, under the provision of the Federal Constitution does authorize the importation of rum and brandy into the State of Maine, and the collection of a duty on the same; how is this inconsistent with the right of the State to prohibit its sale here? The merchant is not obliged to import the article, and if he does, he must take the chance of being able to

vend it. Indeed, it would be a most extraordinary
fact, if in the grants made to the Congress of the
United States the people of the several States had
not reserved sufficient power to provide for their
own internal quiet and security—not sufficient to
regulate or prohibit any traffic which might destroy
the peace and endanger the lives of the citizens.
But it is not necessary to pursue this enquiry, since
the measures proposed by your Committee, are not
justly liable to this objection.

If it is again objected that there is something
stronger and more to be depended on than human
law; even the spread of just sentiments and upright
principles; it may be replied that this is more specious
than sound. For suppose it is true, does it avail in
the present case? The question is not the value of
just sentiment and upright principles, nor the effi-
ciency of controlling the actions of those who possess
those virtues; but it is how men are to be controlled
in the absence of these principles. On what else can
we safely depend but the law, to restrain the vicious
and unprincipled? But the objection before us proves
too much; it proves that we should depend in all other
cases upon just sentiments and upright principles.
Theft and robbery should be restrained in the same
way; and society should be left to the enlightened
consciences of its members for security against injuries
of every kind.

Another objects that we must trust to public opinion
to restrain the traffic. But this is equally visionary
with the other. For public opinion is doubtless now
fixed against highway robbery, but repeal the law

against this crime, and how long could a man travel and be safe? The truth is, laws must be formed for men as they are ; and so long as they are the creatures of passion and appetite, you never will effectually succeed in restraining the perverse and selfish, except by superadding to the dictates of reason. the sanction and authority of law. The question of an essential alteration in the license laws has been canvassed for several years by the people of the State ; and petitions to this effect have been again and again preferred to the Legislature ; and your Committee are of the opinion that the time has arrived when it is proper to act upon the subject ; they therefore offer the annexed Bill.

www.ingramcontent.com/pod-product-compliance
Lightning Source LLC
Chambersburg PA
CBHW021547270326
41930CB00008B/1390